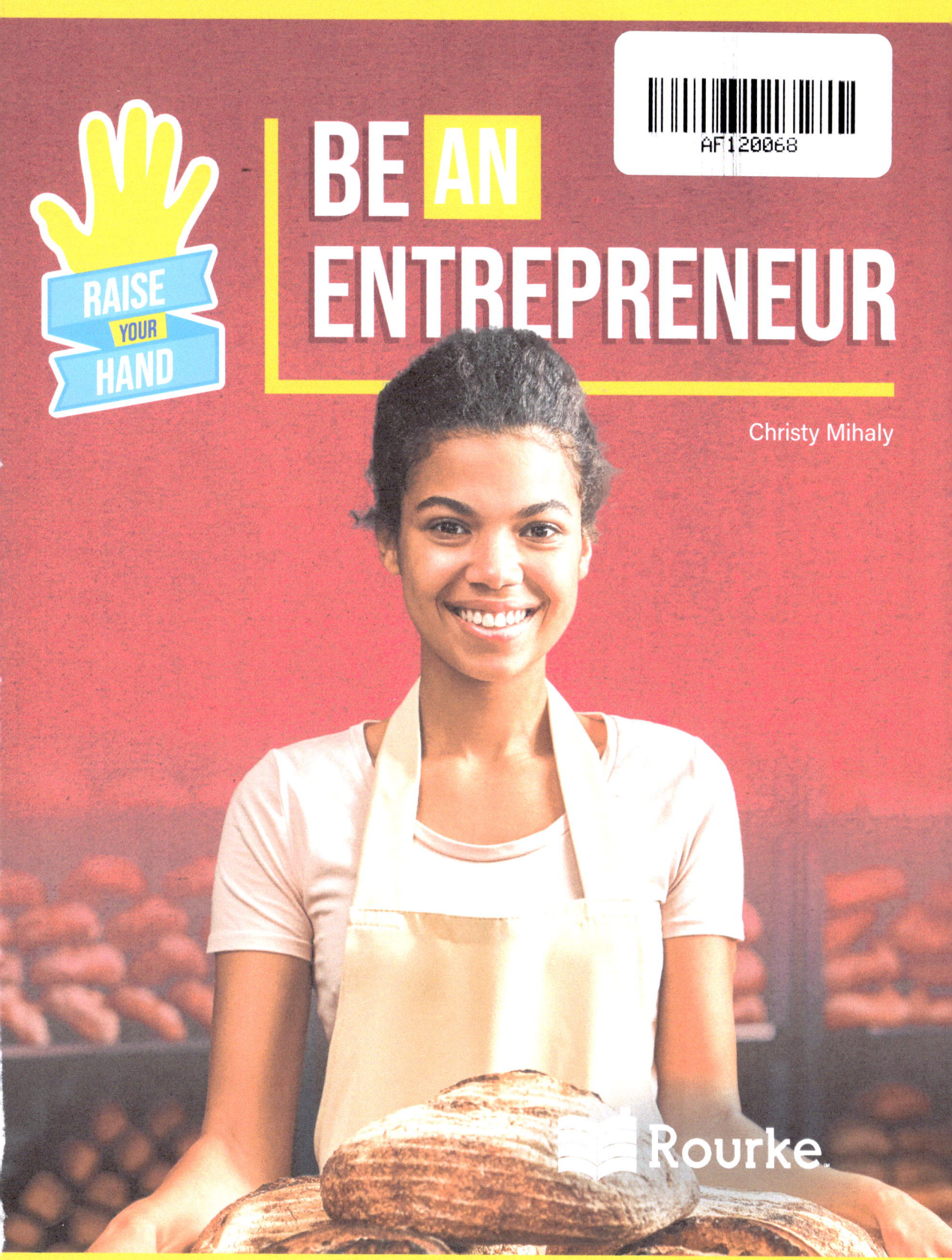

ROURKE'S SCHOOL to HOME CONNECTIONS
BEFORE AND DURING READING ACTIVITIES

Before Reading: *Building Background Knowledge and Vocabulary*

Building background knowledge can help children process new information and build upon what they already know. Before reading a book, it is important to tap into what children already know about the topic. This will help them develop their vocabulary and increase their reading comprehension.

Questions and Activities to Build Background Knowledge:

1. Look at the front cover of the book and read the title. What do you think this book will be about?
2. What do you already know about this topic?
3. Take a book walk and skim the pages. Look at the table of contents, photographs, captions, and bold words. Did these text features give you any information or predictions about what you will read in this book?

Vocabulary: *Vocabulary Is Key to Reading Comprehension*

Use the following directions to prompt a conversation about each word.

- Read the vocabulary words.
- What comes to mind when you see each word?
- What do you think each word means?

Vocabulary Words:
- business plan
- competition
- crowdfunding
- entrepreneur
- genetic
- marketing

During Reading: *Reading for Meaning and Understanding*

To achieve deep comprehension of a book, children are encouraged to use close reading strategies. During reading, it is important to have children stop and make connections. These connections result in deeper analysis and understanding of a book.

Close Reading a Text

During reading, have children stop and talk about the following:

- Any confusing parts
- Any unknown words
- Text to text, text to self, text to world connections
- The main idea in each chapter or heading

Encourage children to use context clues to determine the meaning of any unknown words. These strategies will help children learn to analyze the text more thoroughly as they read. When you are finished reading this book, turn to the next-to-last page for **After Reading Questions** and an **Activity**.

TABLE OF CONTENTS

What Is an Entrepreneur?...........................4
Start with a Problem
    and a Great Idea..12
Make a Plan..20
Memory Game..30
Index..31
After-Reading Questions 31
Activity 31
About the Author 32

WHAT IS AN ENTREPRENEUR?

Entrepreneur? What's that?

An **entrepreneur** is someone who starts a business or organization. But being an entrepreneur means more than that. It means taking risks. It means creating something from an original idea.

When entrepreneurs see problems, they propose solutions. They experiment. They may fail at first, but they keep trying.

entrepreneur (ahn-truh-pruh-NUR): a person who creates and operates a new business and takes risks in doing so

Some entrepreneurs become rich and famous. You've probably heard of Bill Gates, who founded Microsoft. Some are less well known, like Steve

WORM FARM

When ten-year-old Greta Johnson wanted to make money, she started Greta's Worm Farm. She raised worms in bins at home. Greta sold her worms to bait shops. People bought them as bait for fishing.

Chen, Jawed Karim, and Chad Hurley. They started YouTube. Many other entrepreneurs run small businesses, from hot dog stands to toy factories and more.

Successful entrepreneurs make money. But starting a business provides other benefits, too. It offers customers products or services they want. Plus, businesses hire people, giving them jobs.

Different entrepreneurs have different goals. Ayah Bdeir wanted to help young people become inventors and engineers. So, she developed tiny electronic building blocks she called "littleBits" that can be used to make new inventions. Then she started a business to make and sell them. Her goal of encouraging young engineers led her to become an entrepreneur.

When Miles Fetherston-Resch was six years old, he learned how plastic trash in the ocean harms sharks and other animals. He wanted to help. He emptied his piggy bank and sent the money to organizations supporting clean oceans. But it wasn't much. So, Miles started a business to make money. He planned to donate his profits to ocean conservation.

Miles's company, Kids Saving Oceans, sells conservation-themed products, including hats made of recycled plastic from the sea. He sends the profits to groups working to save the ocean. Miles set a goal of donating one million dollars by his eighteenth birthday.

If you want to tackle a big problem—even an oceanic one—put on your entrepreneur's hat and go for it!

START WITH A PROBLEM AND A GREAT IDEA

An entrepreneur sees a problem and comes up with an original idea to solve it. What problem are you facing? Is it that you want to make money? That's a fine place to start.

Now, look for a problem that other people have—something you can fix. Think about your talents, skills, and interests. How can you build on these? That's how entrepreneurs create solutions and profits.

Maybe you know someone who has trouble operating their cell phone or computer. Do you have a knack for technology? This could be your business opportunity.

Would people pay you for tech support? Could you set up and update their phones and computers? What about updating social media or designing websites? Can you think of other possibilities?

AN APP FOR THAT

Jordan Casey, a student in Ireland, got an idea when his teacher lost her notebook. That's where she wrote her class information. Jordan created and sold an app that enables teachers to organize records online.

Maybe you're an expert on something. Think about how you might put your knowledge to work. In 2006, Anne Wojcicki had been studying healthcare. She thought people could stay healthier if they knew more about their **genetic** makeup.

She decided to start a business offering genetic testing to customers. With two partners, Linda Avey and Paul Cusenza, Wojcicki founded 23andMe. It was the first company to sell quick-and-easy DNA testing kits, letting people find out what's in their genes.

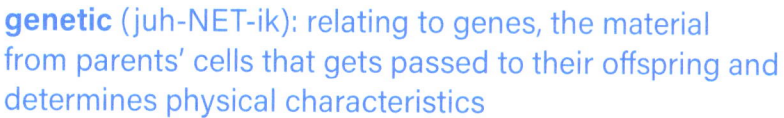

> **genetic** (juh-NET-ik): relating to genes, the material from parents' cells that gets passed to their offspring and determines physical characteristics

If you're a fashionista, maybe you know people who are looking for help finding flattering clothes. Think about turning your fashion sense into a business that helps others find their style.

Artists can be entrepreneurs, too. Look at Beyoncé. Her musical talent helped her launch a multimillion dollar business. She sells many brands and products.

Maybe you can make something that brings people joy. Could you sell your creations? Perhaps you're a musician and could form a band to play at school dances or weddings. Rev up your imagination!

MAKE A PLAN

Once you've spotted a need and developed a solution, it's time to investigate. Can you turn your great idea into a business? Research the **competition**. Is there another business or organization doing what you have in mind? How is your idea different? How can you do better?

Talk with friends and family members. Can they help? Ask experienced businesspeople for their advice.

competition (kahm-puh-TISH-uhn): those attempting to succeed against one another in pursuing a goal

Then, write your **business plan**. Start by identifying your customers. Who will want your product? How will you reach these people? How will you sell to them? This is your **marketing** strategy.

Think about how you'll operate your business. How much time will it take? Will you do it yourself? Will you hire helpers? What will you pay them?

How long do you want to keep your business going? Is it just a summer operation, or year-round? Will you stay in business until you graduate?

business plan (BIZ-nis plan): a proposal laying out a company's goals and a strategy for reaching them

marketing (MAHR-ki-ting): the promoting and selling of products or services

Include expenses in your plan. Calculate the cost of making or providing your product or service. This includes equipment, materials, and paying workers. Add your marketing costs.

What will you charge customers? Calculate your expected income. Consider your costs, prices charged by your competition, and what your customers can afford.

Your plan should show how your business will cover expenses. What's left over is your profit. Will you put your earnings back into your business? When do you expect to make a profit?

GIVING BACK

Some businesses make plans to donate to good causes. Bryan and Bradford Manning are brothers who started the clothing company Two Blind Brothers. They donate one hundred percent of their profits toward curing blindness.

Finally, calculate how much money you need to get started. You'll need to cover initial materials, create a website, and so on. Where will you get these funds? Will you use savings? Will a relative provide a loan?

You might seek other ways to raise funds. Maybe your school has resources for students with business ideas. Community organizations sometimes fund entrepreneurs. Look for contests giving awards to new businesses.

Or consider **crowdfunding**. Often done online, crowdfunding allows supporters to contribute money to get your project started. Contributors might expect a gift in return, such as one of your products. Different platforms work differently, so make sure you're clear about the rules before trying this.

crowdfunding (KROUD-fuhn-ding): raising money through small contributions from many people, usually on the internet

Got your business plan and start-up funds? You're on your way! Remember that being an entrepreneur is hard work. You may not succeed immediately, but entrepreneurs learn from their failures. With a great idea and enough perseverance, you can create something wonderful.

MEMORY GAME

Look at the pictures. What do you remember reading on the pages where each image appeared?

INDEX

Bdeir, Ayah 8
Beyoncé 18
business plan 23, 24, 29
Casey, Jordan 14
expenses 24
Kids Saving Oceans 11
Manning, Bradford and Bryan 24
23andMe 17

AFTER-READING QUESTIONS

1. Name some advantages and some disadvantages of being an entrepreneur.
2. Identify a problem that you could solve or a need you could fulfill by starting a new business.
3. What is a talent or skill that you could use to start your own business?
4. What information should be included in a business plan?
5. Which of the entrepreneurs mentioned in this book do you most admire? Why?

ACTIVITY

Write a business plan for a short-term business you could operate over a school break. For example, you could plan to sell something you make, or offer services such as yard work. Identify a problem or need and your creative solution. In your plan, include what you will sell or provide, your costs, your marketing plan, and how much money you might earn.

ABOUT THE AUTHOR

Christy Mihaly was a lawyer until she went into the business of writing books. She has written more than thirty nonfiction books for young people, including some about turning hobbies into businesses. She believes in the power of raising your hand. She invites readers to visit her website at www.christymihaly.com.

© 2023 Rourke Educational Media

All rights reserved. No part of this book may be reproduced or utilized in any form or by any means, electronic or mechanical including photocopying, recording, or by any information storage and retrieval system without permission in writing from the publisher.

www.rourkebooks.com

PHOTO CREDITS: page 1: ©Viktoriia Hnatiuk/Getty Images, page 4–5: ©THEPALMER/Getty Images; page 6–7: ©Martin Klimek/ZUMAPRESS/Newscom; page 7: ©MediaNews Group/St. Paul Pioneer Press via Getty Images / Contributor; page 8: © (need permission) ; page 8–9: ©AJ_Watt/ Getty Images; page 10–11: © Brandi Image Photography, ©richcarey/ Getty Images; page 12–13: ©SDI Productions/ Getty Images; page 12–13: ©SDI Productions/ Getty Images; page 14–15: ©iammotos/ Getty Images; page 16–17: ©Tim Wagner/ZUMAPRESS/Newscom; page 17: ©David Bro/ZUMA Press/Newscom; page 19: ©Image Press Agency/Sipa USA/Newscom; page 20–21: ©SDI Productions/ Getty Images; page 22–23: ©Michael Blann/ Getty Images; page 24: ©(need permission); page 24–25: ©ljubaphoto/Getty Images; page 26–27: ©Ryan McVay/Getty Images; page 28–29: ©chingyunsong/Getty Images; page 30:©Photography by Adri/Getty Images, ©richcarey/ Getty Images, ©Tim Wagner/ZUMAPRESS/Newscom, Image Press Agency/Sipa USA/Newscom, ©Michael Blann/ Getty Images, ©Ryan McVay/Getty Images

Edited by: Laura Malay
Cover and interior design by: Nick Pearson

Library of Congress PCN Data

Be an Entrepreneur / Christy Mihaly
(Raise Your Hand)
ISBN 978-1-73165-289-8 (hard cover) (alk. paper)
ISBN 978-1-73165-259-1 (soft cover)
ISBN 978-1-73165-319-2 (e-book)
ISBN 978-1-73165-349-9 (e-pub)
Library of Congress Control Number: 2021952174
Rourke Educational Media
Printed in the United States of America
02-0202313053